DIMINUTIVE REVOLUTIONS

DANIEL BOUCHARD

SUBPRESS BOOKS

2000

Some poems first appeared in *Bivouac, Boog Literature, Compound Eye, The Boston Poet, The End Review, The Hat, The Impercipient, Kenning, Mass Ave., Mirage#4/Period(ical),* and *Poetry New York.*

Wrackline was first published by Situations Press, New York City, 1999.

Cover design by O'Connor & Price Design.

ISBN: 0-9666303-9-4

Subpress Collective and 'A 'A Arts
2955 Dole Street
Honolulu, Hawai'i 96816

CONTENTS

WRACKLINE

A red-winged blackbird on gray
fence post spreads wings and
sings into wind. A hill
behind shacks, sloping to salt marsh
I walk in late afternoon. The sun
ignites mosses, lichens, grasses
very dry, soft to lay on. Scotch pines,
decades old, the soft hillside of rotten
branches and pine needles.
On the drive to work
I sometimes see K getting coffee
at a donut shop. There is a cemetery
across the street from a hamburger place.
My friend Ed is buried there.
Crumpled ironing boards, new cardboard
boxes, their tight interior
styrofoam, paper envelopes, paper
towels, paper napkins, paper
cups, cans emptied of vegetables,
soda, soup and beer.
Truck routes rotate every day;
assigned to three, twice a week
I do two. Nuthatch, wren, and woodthrush.
I learn the truck routes by rote. They digress
in a labyrinth of back roads and side streets.
Paper plates, plastic forks, wine
bottles, old clothing, plastic
that wrapped new things.
To emerge onto a main road
means significant ground has been covered,

to emerge onto a main road
in the direction opposite from that
which you first came means the day
is winding down. Containers, stuff
from bathrooms, stuff from kitchens
all heaved into the truck. Salt
spray rose, sassafras.
Black cherry, bear berry, seaside
goldenrod, sea beach sandwort.
Morning comes and the pillow
cools quickly after your face leaves it.
In early summer work hours are shorter
though the days are longer.
Lilac bushes border the lots
of neatly trimmed lawns. Green water
at low tide, the flats at Brewster.
American goldfinch trio flies
at truck noise. Route 6, also
"Grand Army of the Republic Highway"
is quiet and empty at sunrise. A bicyclist
headed north, preceded by a small car
acting as windbreak in narrow lane
right of the white line.
Mayflower, starflower,
the vulnerable broom crowberry.
Ed was killed in a car wreck,
thrown from the passenger seat.
Meadowsweet.
Twisted pitch pine
in patches. Northern cardinal
coming at me above wooded path
of crushed clamshells. I tear open
a bag, find a box of seeds, open the box

and scatter the remnants in wind,
watch while we move fast away from them.
After the interment of his body
we left the cemetery and crossed the street
to the burger place where the mood
lightened considerably.
Pickerelweed. The alewives
at Brewster swim upstream.
The seeds fall in the road, blow
among grasses and weeds, drop
onto lawns, into pavement cracks,
into a creek we speed over
on a low built bridge. Two years later
I was living a short distance north of his grave.
I shake the box over the road and toss it
back into the truck. Newspapers, magazines,
books, plastic oil quarts and milk cartons.
We swim in kettle ponds after the beach.
Pipsissewa. Broken garden gear,
things from the garage
or backyard. Green-winged teal
and gadwall. Hot sand, hot asphalt,
wet sand, shaded asphalt, the cool grasses
of green lawns almost as good as
standing in the ocean
or the clumped, dry grasses of unmowed
fields, sharp or soft.
Bayberry, beach pea, beach
plum and highbrush blueberry.
In June I dream the new job dream
of repetitive motion: tossing bags
into the truck pit, holding on
to outside handles, jumping

from the truck as it slows.
The clean, clear, very cold water
of kettle ponds, the sloping bottom
descends into deeper blue, the water
grows cooler as you swim down.
Golden heather. The dream
reconfigures in different places:
mixing shellfish in cornmeal batter
and buttermilk before dropping
them into a deep fryer, shoveling
gravel, roller painting, removing
sanitized dishes from a rack, or driving
for long stretches at a time (in the dream
my foot presses pedals).
Sanderlings.
My ankles crack like splitting quahogs.
Rockweed. Brian said
it's toughest in winter,
the stops infrequent but the weather
severe. Belted kingfisher and
hairy woodpecker.
The Franklin wrecked at Cahoon Hollow
in 1848. No maggots in winter. That's
when it's easy, he said, to sit down
halfway through a route and roll a joint.
Thoreau visited the oysterman's house
at Gull Pond; today the steep hills are dense
with growth. The dogs dig holes
in the sandy yard. Pine needles stick
in foot. Sand spills
onto pavement of parking lots,
over concrete curbs, tar soaked utility poles.
Cordgrass.

Small cement trash pit covered
by foot-levered steel top
in yards of older houses. A sign
warns against visual impairment
in sandstorms. Asleep at midnight
on a Commercial Street stoop
intoxicated by slummy New England
proper nouns, not used to long work hours.
Beer and tomato juice make a red-eye.
Eastern meadowlark. Oil leaks
onto the road, onto the driveway,
dirt and sand, all over the engine, drips
onto hot parts, burning and smoking, I smell
behind the wheel. From work I take a bike,
push-mower, books, refundable
cans and bottles, fishing lures, art,
a dealer-issued car stereo,
unopened beer and soda, pornography,
bric-a-brac, old photographs, appliances.
I wrecked the rusting diesel Rabbit
on the hilly road approaching Sagamore
Bridge three weeks after buying it. The car
pulls out of a lot on the right and pauses.
Storms in the southwestern sky, roads
suddenly empty so when
birds fly into the tree line they appear
to move quicker than usual, as if
evasively. Pine needles pushed
aside in hard rain clumped together
in green pools of pollen. Welded handles
back of the truck betray in bright metal
a legacy of my predecessors. European starlings
efficiently strip the landscape,

driving out other birds. The smashed
but salvageable front end: I reconnect the battery
cables, tie down the hood, brush shattered plastic
from the bumper, and drive off.
Cedar waxwing. Wainscoting
in heaps by the house being redone.
I look at pushpin and tack holes,
cover it when the compact kicks in
and hear the wood snap in a sharp
hydraulic crush. The Cape
is one big aquifer. Diesel in the morning
mixes like a chemical solution
of sea brine and pine trees off the back
of a garbage truck at six A.M.
From a wrecked Rabbit on the company lot
I take the hood, plastic grille, headlight casings,
antenna and right side fender. Bees had made
a home by the engine. What was the monster
Thoreau thought watched him from the water
as he walked the beach? Crow's roadside vigil.
I like old houses on the Cape that create
a settled landscape. Fireflies. A cedar tree
or pine grove in the yard. Dormer windows
open to ocean breeze. Mansard roof,
widow's walk. We feed carrots to horses
at the fence along the driveway, they learn
to expect us Tuesday mornings, waiting and
disappointed if we forget carrots,
so we give them whatever we have
when we have no carrots. Pine
warbler, prairie warbler
and yellow warbler.
Maggots collect in water

slide with garbage bits
and scum down the steel slope.
Tires swish, racing on unpeopled roads in rain.
The water under the drain hole
collects in the trash pit and sloshes
while we drive, splashing us. We climb
atop the Provincetown water tower
on a clear night—stars, a semicircle of lights
to the west beyond the bay,
north to the bridge, we see clearly,
along Plymouth and the South Shore
coastal towns, a brilliant glow above Boston,
the rim of a bowl, and in the center, black
water. Poverty grass. The dogs get skunked,
need a tomato juice bath. As Thoreau and
Channing were leaving, the oysterman
(who claimed he heard Bunker Hill guns
across the bay as a boy) asked them the names
of things in his garden
grown with seeds gathered from wrecked ships.
Sunday mornings the drive-in lot
is a flea market and on Mondays we collect
the vendors' overstock. Cabbage, broccoli
and parsley. Even the thrift shop
throws things away, a blue dumpster
stuffed with clothes and housewares.
On Pleasant Bay after work we motor a dingy
to the boat and speed out to deeper water
where Brian rigs a line for me.
The lure is lost on the cast.
Tim hooks two striped bass.
Brian rigs me another line. We bake the fish,
eat it with rice and cold beer

on the couch watching *Apocalypse Now,*
afterward get so stoned I can't drive home
and crash on the living room floor.
Stay off the dunes. A small beagle
tied up in a yard so anticipates our arrival
we hear his bark two streets away.
He looks, as we grab his owner's trash,
he will burst waiting to be pet, which I do
while the truck turns. I rub his head, neck,
kneading his ears, down his spine, oily coat,
he rolls on his back, I rub his belly, his tongue
hangs out, I run for the truck, the beagle
barks after me, tail wagging, straining his
length of leash. Cowbird in puddle
holds bug in beak. All the Cape they say,
will vanish, like Billingsgate Island
once 60 acres (houses, meadows, schools,
church) submerged to 5 acres to mud flats
to sandbank to sea.

sand
scrub pine
sand

sky

sand dunes blue water
green beach grass white sand blue
shoal water

breakers wet white sand

horizon

sun bleach wood white clouds

sea straw white sand, white crest lip
daylight moon

sand, water, sky and yellow line
black asphalt lot surrounded
by parabolic dunes

A common loon. Sand
stuck to feet and feet to cool
tessellated rubber, gas and clutch
the car is hot when opened but cools
driving winding roads, windows down,
toward town, fresh skin burn in sea air.
Piping plovers pick at a poppy seed
bagel in the parking lot. Truck snaps
tree limbs on tight corners of private roads.
No-see-ums frenzy before morning heat
or cool of late afternoon. Squirrels, raccoons,
opossum, frogs, turtles, birds,
snakes crushed against road.
Brushed off the truck, I try to skedaddle
toward the back, moving at a good clip
on a beach road, branches
combing the cable laden sides
of the wide truck, and nearly fell under.
I roll to avoid rear wheels.
Cranberry bogs darken to crimson.
Roseate tern. A ring
of brambles around the bog,
beyond dirt road tall trees darkened green.
Maggots have a distinct smell.

They lay eggs in early morning, the sloppy
trail visible across black or green plastic bags.
Eider, osprey and hawk.
The smell of diesel in afternoon
dissipated by pavement heat.
Beach grass thrives under layers of sand
and its own yellowed stalks. White oak.
Sand fleas and tiger beetles. Names painted
or engraved onto expensive varnished wood
or slate: "Linger Longer," "Remembrance,"
"Big Sky," "Break Away," "Our Hide A Way."
The smell of pot drifts on beach
from vague direction. Poison ivy. In tides
torn kelp and shattered shells surround
the battered wreck of a pop can. Dogshit
proliferates, dries, decays and blows away.
From the beach: freighters, tankers,
trawlers, draggers, liners. Monday mornings
we empty the enormous condo sheds
south of 6A. Brian imitates our boss,
an ex-Marine officer who speaks Vietnamese,
with an energy burst grabbing seven bags,
running to the truck shouting nonsense
in a mock-Asian inflection. Running back,
grabs metal tops, slams them on empty
pails and still shouting moves down the line.
Afterward we eat pancakes at a diner,
pancakes every time. My work gloves
tattooed magic marker surface
tattered completely by close of summer.
Monkfish is known as poor man's lobster,
sometimes goosefish disguised; hence goosefish
is poor, unsuspecting man's monkfish.

16

All their plans and hopes burst like a bubble!
said Thoreau of the immigrant shipwreck
victims whose corpses he saw at Cohasset.
Iraq invades Kuwait on a Thursday.
The fuel line rubber lining melted twice
because I couldn't feel the capless tube
releasing hot air. In a formal picture
Ed stands with friends in a white suit.
Depleted plutonium becomes a military
recycling success. I like the sober statements
of age and matrimony
engraved under angelic skulls
on the old slate tombstones of colonial villages.
Heatwince beside idling truck
as its vapors pass over skin.
Bluejays on bench, new boards bolted and
painted red. Marsh leaves and twigs
blowing past truck side, my hands
in canvas gripped to steel bars,
leaning into wind,
my face burned by sun.

AUGUST

So came August to its close
—Henry Beston

I

And then we burned all the ships
set oil into breakers

Even a few stories

An order, formal in its
aloofness

Ground detachment, an
observation
of subjective administration

Of flow,
people, vehicles, birds and
energy on the conduit surface
across the planet

And pavement signs posted
tinnily into streets

II

The hand
and

the metal band about the bone
mixes dough in the plastic bowl

Metallurgical seasons

Fastidious

Flat skyscrapers in the day's last light

A history not of attention but
the remnants of that attention
charactered
after a fashion

Someday I wish to wring lilies from the acorn

      III

The bus and the bug
straight thru the neighborhood

A parabola of perception
A concavity of glass

        From within
the sight thru the windshield
the TV reception without
focus, the closing second
half of the twentieth the waning
twentieth century

IV

The structure does or may
withstand
much that is not
intent

Stand on the beach long enough
it will in time wipe you away
in time coasts cut away, the time
coasts take to form, is it
create or destroy?

This is all reordered fact
barring all that
which is not recorded

This recognition poetry produces

And produces
at intervals

V

Liftoff.
Amazing.
Somebody sure was
using their head here. The plane
rises above land that once was
Boston Harbor. Clouds soon obscure the earth.

Above

Jersey coastline, the pilot announces
Atlantic City
and indeed a beach metropolis
and the jugular highway I almost got killed on
three summers ago
situated and slipping by
implacably below me.

A paper thin projection of history
safety in certainty
and certainly knowledge

But to move really move in a lifetime
a reservoir of uncertainty to press
any force other
than your own which is all
one can answer for
to the self
or another

From the air the suburbs clearly show
true petroleum dependence.
A cul-de-sac scratched out
in a pasture

Topography of a sprawling world

All in all everything from this height
even the industries look
to be in perfect order

The plane touches down
on the day of Marie's wedding.
Ten years ago I took a train
and got off at 30th Street Station.

Philadelphia heat wave
stifling August coming home
electric up the west highway
beside the Schuylkill.

Dave, Rob, Rich
are all married now.

That biologic inertia
radial lives   a myriad graph of
heartbeats:
sex, sweat,
eat, work and sleep
                          The pulse beat
periodic pull
when drawn
draws intervals together

A photograph from the paper: July 4, 1985
big concert, big summer crowd
swells the streets of the Parkway

Attendance in a pitch of season
the bay isles in the backyard

Shots of tequila past midnight

VI

A pavement ontology
at this point
pin point

yet ample time
which fills all time or

all the time one may have.

The night of my cousin's wedding and the night
or rather, morning
the students of Tiananmen Square are slaughtered
like bothersome pests in the basement

We watch the cable transmission, the blood
runs in the streets
and the government steals the corpses
and there is nothing
anyone
can do
about it

A shoe on the step

The sun

Wind

A small spider struggles
against dust filaments on the wall

VII

In the company of women
the women whose
company I enjoy

Friends many years we
have more past in common than
the future promises

Street-car, train, trolley
electric clack across the city surface
swallowed by and
spit out tunnels

The absorbed people
entranced by the words
of advertisements, newspapers, novels and reports.
Never forget the words of good-time Walt:
If you meet some stranger in the streets and love him or her,
why I often meet strangers in the street and love them.

Siren approach and fade

The garbage pickers of my world
are not those of Robert Lowell's
tho Marlborough Street has changed little

VIII

The bend in the trail
a wash in the water

Awake to the vagaries of sentiment
that lastly lag along these beach roads

Water washes off the car in
an engineer's streamlined gutter

A little learning is a complacent thing.
Porter beer. Sourdough bread.
The trumpet
of Kenny Dorham.
Letters from Maryland
come up the coast.

Life must be at least as well lived as fantasy

Cooped in mnemonics
weeks fold upon each other

Daylight fades. Mosquitoes invade
the picnic strewn
across the lawn

                    IX

A great body of black water.
The ocean at midnight defined by sound,
starlight and porch lights from
the houses on the hill. The sky
and us, the waves drift
thru us,
small waves

the waves
smack
our bodies
in darkness, small
kisses,
warm summer.
Your warm skin tastes of salt.

X

Mosses and lichens
in the woods of Wellfleet

Recreate prudently, the president advises
and the motors hum far off the coast

A summer to write about

In the closet of the cottage
a tiny toad hides
under a laundry pile.
We capture
to release it outside.

XI

Malcolm X meets
Big Bill Haywood

Streetlights coming on

XII

Muffled shouts of neighbors

Boston is dank
and dirty like a drained fish tank

Skateboard kids learn
their skateboard skill

Boylston Street at five

Someday anthropologists will discover the car alarm
and realize how ridiculous we are,
but they will note seeing-eye dogs
and know how ingenious we could be

Stability or engineering
erring

The suitability street corner
of time

A place set

The dinner on the table

XIII

*Copyrights are required for book production in the United
States. However, in our case, it is a disliked necessity.*

This is the world on fire   flame sold separately

Real heat creeps
into the season   the sun seen from an open door
of the crawling commuter train

These things here long
before and long after:
         arranged stones, poetry,
plutonium,
oceans and tapestry

Nuclear waste, he says! Eye-roll
annoyance

Never forget the words of ponderous Walt:
how often I thought of you, ages and ages hence

and the poisoned world
you will choke in

         XIV

Little will, little or
little else
the life span of sparrows

The metal about the bone
The engravement on the stones

One hot stretch of summer
skin burned in the breeze

oil leak, the seas
theatric tantric

A change in the weather

XV

In dry night a thunderhead explodes

The heavy bass keys of an organ
all at once
an electric hum rolls in the sky and

vibrates the walls of the house

Sunday nights ebb away I think
of all I have
not done, read, seen

Stop this day and night with me

Repossess the means

A PAVEMENT ONTOLOGY

Stir.
Black.
Loam in a fist-sized pot.
The bread is warm
and lovely. A thin straw
swirls and leans on
a ceramic rim.
Traffic waves. A throat
pulse, Pennsylvania
morning, October in your
room that was months ago.
Sandpiper tag after. Moonrise
over a black bay.
A new summer means
a new address. I saw you
at a streetcar stop this morning.
Rainy days and Mondays, etc.
There are no birds in Boston
like on the coast of Rhode Island.
I wanted to believe it was you.
I think little of highways,
of Pennsylvania roads.
Most of it I remember. Your hair,
your hands, the fact you couldn't run well.
You look so pretty in a dress.
And softly said 'Dear heart how like you this?'

To walk out from the building
the morning after
an intense rainstorm and discover
a car crushed by a last-century tree

at a Philadelphia intersection.
Your skin
is warm and lovely. This
was all farmland once.

AT THE INTERSECTION OF ROTHSCHILD AND OLSON

The glint of streetlights
reflects off moving cars,
and in the lot frozen flakes
like cake frosting stick
from Sunday's snow squall.
The blue electric light on the insurance tower
means clear weather ahead, and the coffee
dust on the formica top,
pressboard and sheet metal
table behind me means
I'm a slob. Clean daylight is
burning and drops off
behind the series of high-rise public housing
set up now for profit
at private ownership.

Around a bend of the Charles
an embankment (100 years old)
holds me
as I walk looking at Venus, Jupiter
and the red blur which is Mars
and if I live to be a hundred won't see
this alignment again
tho I cannot see much now
thru the water
lenses in my eyes.
                    At the flat of Alexia Hayes
I give a simple assessment of books.
She's no Melville spinster
possessing literary ephemera

but bent and old sells her beloved library
to pay creditors off
cashing in on her eviction.

O, Charles Olson, what wide thoughts I have of you tonight!
Shall we type the sun down, go out smoke-walking at one A.M.,
and pee off the municipal pier? The light in here
getting brighter, your fat book
in the clearing of the table.
If I love it, why do I rail against it?
Its precise best reminds me
of Douglas' poems: *two thicknesses*
of glass windows
who between me
and the outside, trying to see actual flakes.

WASHINGTON SQUARE

Quick roads thru the country.
Driven impressions
we arrive at
the centuries' intricate layers
the driven shoots
the respite of space
the city between
complex geometries.
The architecture progresses.
Churns of renewal
like generations. Nostalgia
cannot prevent it.

Hot summer. Where was you at?
That great brick grid if
under the sun at all
will not and cannot remember.

Days of vilification
not glory. It is the place
always the place we live.
Temerity and passion
unknown to the landscape.

Remember
that girl you met one night
dining out alone?
Summer past, summer next.
At the end of every July I intend
to write a poem called
August.

The parks persist in form.
Houdon's *Washington*
above the fire that burns
thru recurrent wars. People
drift in pockets to read
words, hands in pockets
or arms crossed, read silently

FREEDOM IS A LIGHT FOR WHICH
MANY MEN HAVE DIED
IN DARKNESS

or so the ad man said
when they dug up
some One
in the 1950s.

John Adams wrote home:

"enough to make the Heart of stone
to melt away. The Sexton told me,
upwards of two Thousand soldiers
had been buried there, and
by the Appearance, of the Graves,
and Trenches, it is most probable to me
he speaks within Bounds."

All of this is yours
to ignore. The street trash
vanishes eventually
on the streets of Philadelphia.

By the water once
a wave of clouds
eclipsed the sun and I
beheld green water
free of glare. The colors
and the texture and the vista
made perfect sense
in a perfect light.

Those people with you then
now also on their way
the numbered streets west
past great buildings, miles
and miles
the great box-like empty buildings
of busted windows
and rust stained ledges.
The stones accrue a heavy moss.

In my mind's eye
I see the city's length
as entering from the north
beside the south running river.
Under the girders
of the quick highway not
so long ago. Lyme
and mortar. Add
and delete. On the pavement
now and again
the realization
materializes:
the filial breadth of one's commitment.

LINES NOT DEDICATED

SPACE WITHIN THESE

I

The neighborhood of early Congress

appearances at work
    apparent in the architecture

structures meant to be
    looked at.

Appellative morning
                        new day

                a sense of the city, utility
        preconceived

here or near

            4th │ &
        ────────┼──────
                │ Filbert

Aggregation
    an accumulation
        of matters

privilege and
    content, unrequited mass

"it's a nice walk
    but the way to the water is
        hindered by the highway"

37

no ships, few
cars, drone
of plane engines.

What remittance
        the idea of *private law*

—in common citizenry
  a Republic—

        a code among the initiated,
stature, elevation

II

Work, sleep/ death

Build you a city round this

Play, eat/ sleep

Friends organize
or attempt to organize
their lives as a series
of ends by means,
gathered round diversions
    or entertainments.

When I seek clarity   when I seek form

appropriation of materials
    is a poly-lane highway.

III

Whole trees, branches
  frozen over

(bronzed whips
        stone wind)

sidewalks
  unwalkable

side slides, how
easily commerce
  unmercifully ceases

the goods/ the foods

a halcyon ice holiday
holy Thursday ice age
of poetry and power

secular liturgical slip,
the city is solid
slid to a stop.

IV

Assembling old bones
  chiseled from dry clay.

Contemporary
  proverbial

"who gives a shit"

("I" sayeth the incontinent one)

I can no more avoid political concerns than
I can avoid the fact it's snowing outside.

I'm trying to think
   not narrate—
      I'll tell you about it later.

Reading Terminal   questionable end
I'd have bought the ticket
roadways mend   a past supper
ampersand ampersand ampersand
animated talk   Dirty Frank's
beside the fixtures   outside the toil
the stately bank   the coffee shop
icy curbstones   neon juke
strangers are people in context inside
smell of cigarettes   smell of beer
property rests in geography's realm
Hamilton Burr Van Buren Monroe
intransigent snow   sky is demure
checks cashed   the billion, million
I haven't a quarter for Illinois Jacquet
global turning   the neighborhood of now
market inner winter city
the easy meander of our nomenclature
co-opts what the camera cannot capture

PAX

I make a pact with you, Ron Silliman—
I have admired your poetry long enough.
I came to you as a prodigal pup
Weaned at a dozen fat anthologies.
I am old enough now to make an end.
Whitman broke the new wood,
Pound put in time to carving.
We watch the blasted stumps in the open fields
Leak black ink of American grain.

I make a pact with you, venerable LangPoets—
I have studied your works long enough.
I look back at you as a honorable bunch
Laying new asphalt over the old roads;
I am old enough now to map an end.
It was you who splintered the carved wood,
Now is a time for recycling.
We have a cool climate and a rich soil—
Don't let the mulcher come between us.

I make a pact with you, my contemporaries—
For to know you better there is time enough.
I come to you with no gifts
But that of mutual comradeship;
I am ready to make friends.
Look around us at all this damned wood,
Now is the time to sort out what you want.
We have glasses of water nursing new roots—
Let there be communication between us.

A Private History of Books

The red line is the fastest line of the four subway lines
and I enter a block from my apartment in Cambridge
Central Square where the building that housed the radical
bookshop is vacant, awaiting destruction, being held up
by groups who protested its demise but in the end
failed. The reason actually it hasn't been wrecked yet
is that the Eviction Free Zone objected to a special permit
requested by the owner and biggest landlord in the city
(after Harvard) who wanted to add more apartments
onto the back. In this building, where CVS wants to move,
low-income tenants won two bitter rent strikes over a period of three years,
but the landlord, whose time is devoted exclusively
to devising strategies for higher profits and legal methods
of retaliation, eventually evicted all the tenants
one by one. Until he, the landlord, decides to withdraw his request
or find a loophole through new construction permits
the city block will remain standing, and Central Square
will have to wait for high-rise luxury housing and superfluous
chain stores at the ground level. The radical bookshop
is named for an activist who was also married to one
of the Haymarket Martyrs. It's a rare bookshop anywhere
where you can find out who the Haymarket Martyrs were,
especially in the bookshops open on May Day and Labor
Day, which means practically all of them. Once when
Douglas came to visit he boasted that a bookshop
near his house in Brooklyn was more radical than any other
bookshop. He meant the Pathfinder which is quite
selective in what they sell, which is what they publish,
which does not divert from a particular political line
which is all fine but not very radical. They are fine

for speeches of Debs, Malcolm X, things by Trotsky
but not Gramsci or Goldman, Mother Jones or Voltairine de Cleyre.
Or Kropotkin either although I did find once
at the 'oldest, continuous, antiquarian bookshop'
with the misleading name named for a city square
torn down for new government buildings a copy
of the anarchist prince's memoirs published
by a prestigious Boston publisher. They
were first serialized in a prestigious
Boston monthly, and had it been only two years
later (or, in the wake of Czolgosz killing McKinley)
surely never would have been printed. The steel
engravings inside are fine, with a beautiful frontispiece
preserved by paper film. The book stood on the dollar
rack and my heart leaped to find it. You can't find it
in a library and the only alternative is to pay twenty dollars
for a paperback from Canada, and while that particular press
is a good press to support, nineteen dollars goes a long way
still for a young poet. The narrative alone is worth far more
than a dollar and there is room enough in my world,
altho not room enough in my apartment, for luxurious
cheap old books on good paper that fill my head.
The danger of dollar racks lies in picking things up
you don't want, don't need and will read only
from a single, certain angle on the shelf but who
can place a money value on books besides the dealers
who carry shopping bags filled with first editions
to poetry readings and talk the poet up
while the poet signs high price increases
into otherwise affordable editions. I watched a bookseller once
whose shop is behind the Arlington Street Church
ask John Ashbery to sign no less than fifteen books. He did,
sweet man that he is. They're are all so obliging:

Robert Creeley, Noam Chomsky, but not
writers below a certain age say under thirty in 1960.
With each John Hancock John Ashbery put
another volume out of my price range.
Rare book dealers are the landlords of literature.
Ron Silliman I think is conscious of this price gouging
and someone told me he doesn't sign books but he did
for me once in Philadelphia when I came from Boston
to hear him read with Lyn Hejinian. He walked away from me
inspecting the book and the underlined passages. Finally
he signed it with his e-mail address and not
a signature. The dollar Kropotkin cannot be measured
nor the George Eliot set which was once owned
by Esther Campbell Goodwin, received as a gift
from Harriet L. Goodwin in 1899—a green cloth,
gold finished twenty-two volume set set in the sun
at a buck a piece because one volume was missing.
Same for a set of Cowper's life and letters
they have beautiful typeface and bindings
and illustrations so impractical and fine
who cares if the Brattle's staff is rude? Booksellers
everywhere are rude except where they are interested.
Sven and I once listened in Cambridge to a bookseller
accost a customer when the customer wanted cash
for his old books. The bookseller lit into him, gave him
a lengthy lecture on the economics of running a bookstore
and advised him to open his own. Then the bookseller
looked over the pile while the customer backed away.
I trust you, he said, which inflamed the bookseller again: why
trust me! he demanded and insisted the customer stay put
but in the end he got a good price
for his old paperbacks because he had cared
for their condition. That's the bookstore in the basement

that doesn't set high prices on first editions
nevermind rare ones. And Ange once found a copy
of Bernadette Mayer's *Midwinter Day* there. Since then
I look at the M's first in the poetry section but a duplicate
copy has never appeared. It's in bulk you find things
worthwhile: the person who unloaded the excellent collection
of 1960s poetry paperbacks I followed into the store
within hours. That was a Donald Allen Black Mountain haul
of long out-of-print verse. And the little Black
Sparrow wrapped in boards with Oppen's signature in the back
for a few bucks. And the seven or so Allen Ginsberg
chapbooks scooped up a few months before he died.
Larry Price came to Cambridge, and we stood in my apartment
where the ceiling had yellowed and the wet plaster still stunk
from where the rain pooled and leaked. Don't he said get rid of any
books. None. He did so to regret it once before traveling.
I cannot follow his advice but his tone stuck.
It's easy to trade books you will read only once,
or not at all, like advance copies that arrive at work
unsolicited, misaddressed, and dull (*The Evolving
Rationality of Rational Expectations*). Let the
rational buy it for half price and the bookseller give me
twenty per cent the publisher's price for store credit. I'm happy,
I picked up Paz's *La estación violenta* for five dollars.
It's not that the bookseller doesn't know the real (but inflated)
value of this *primera edición*, Mexico City 1958,
he doesn't care to be troubled
so he tells me. It's the rare book
dealers who call themselves rare book dealers
one should be wary of, looking for the big find
as on Wall Street buy low sell high.
It's strange how peaceful sensations
elicited sometimes by dry planks

serving as shelves where bookmarks
of other used shops are pasted
which are only nudges upon proclivity
of restlessness stir images, thought and
imagination otherwise left alone or
at least not often associated with
where you're at right now
like sex the funniest memories
spring upon the mind
when the mind is not necessarily needed.
Places you haven't been to in years, things
you haven't remembered in years.
Ephemera too sets that off
even postcards of streets you never have known
of horse-cars, economies, costumes
you never knew or information into
worlds you never knew, a curbstone
placement present today
accommodating then
an alley now absent. It's the map
lines so thin I can reasonably distinguish
the eastern shore of Aquidneck Island
only six inches from the Hudson Bay.

LATE WINTER

In late winter Thoreau
managed only *purple finch*
upon the page.
Color in fusion
configures a glimpse
or glare in streetcar window.

Sidewalks creep back over
the road (a kind of civic moss).
Nightclub avenue, steel gate
storefronts; the place changes again.
Next to model streetscapes,
a wide river
on photo grid precision.
Forty years ago progress meant
wider streets downtown.

Light drizzle soaks the square,
darkens mineral bits of pavement
and the sea brine smells like life itself.

Clipped steps of hurried people. A gait
of sanguine insanity they look
so unsettled in so natural an act.
Streetcars race beside outbound traffic
and a hundred red lights brighten in sync.

A Lexicon Is Part of Declarative Memory

A wildflower
The lily past
Days of anemone yore

Past bloom of your asphodel
Buttercup days of old
Days past of old lily in the valley

Days grace gone cranes bill by
Old flower desire of butterfly bygone days
The golden old tulip days

Heyday roses, geranium gorgeousness,
auld lang syne begonia, marigold
antiquity, remote nasturtium

Peacock garden age
Windflower gloss
Magnificence

An Indoctrination Into the Nervous System

Closed windows of parked cars glare
Beneath airborne, metallic, peripheral wings
Fine light flashes in rapid synapse, a moment ago
There, a tiny white dot of seabird on the water.
Under iceberg clouds set free in summer
The flashes pass like a silent pack
of firecrackers on blacktop lot, a twenty-thousand foot drop
Where scale increases on this weekday afternoon.
No cars now but a young woman with a camera
To her eyes, what eyes I think, she aims into the
Bushes maybe at birds with a flush of indigo or scarlet
Brushed wings. Not scarlet now but cranberry,
Russet and dark heavy green, the terrain
Between thin lines of gray road etched along the coast,
Purple sea, its sand lipped shore, steep grade,
Surface wrinkled like a skin susceptible to puncture.

HESIOD'S NOTEBOOK

Under the Emperor Shi Hwang Ti
rose the Great Wall of China
in a remarkable book burning era.
Those pliant skies are indebted
to a majestic reckoning grace. Traffic
proceeds. Roots thicken and stem
into highway system. Grasses drawn
crack up the concrete, pavement rifts
and narrow seams of curb.

Dreaming I read while I sleep
the landscape passes beside the highway
my mood in tandem with a poet's book.
Urban storefront shop: chunk lite tuna,
49 cents. Light in March. Morning
by streetcar rail. Imagine there's no Lenin,
it isn't hard to do. Reminder: Fitz Hugh
Lane remainder, six bucks. Under the
overpass by rail. The indemnity for structures
torn down and hauled away. Sincerity
is blues that stays blues. Sun above sill
reaches refuse: pasta box,
sauce jar, wine bottle and beer
can. To live with friends or amongst them?
Reconnaissance when first consonants fail.
Jet fuel flows with ground water. Tomato,
avocado, and cucumber sandwich.
In twin signatures, graffiti and advertising
what else bearing in civic instruction
is the obsequious city written out?

I have wasted time in sunlight's vanity.
If you would like to make a speech
press pound now.

Dust motes seen at sun's insistence.
Swift's ancestral men retain an unspeakable language.
I see the day's ceaseless consistency
as sea waves compile an enduring
and lasting testimony:
scalloped   reverberate
W I T H D R A W A L
By the Bulfinch prison the river is heavy
with hepatitis after a rain.
A great blue heron lights from the water's edge.
Two Japanese maples wrapped in burlap by the coast.
Spring comes and only deters us.
Birds are great but *the ideal is a flower*
whose root lies in the material conditions of existence.
Sea lavender, larkspur and heather find
my affection for a place. Great
Canadian geese fly in formation over the city.
The feds failed to deport John Lennon,
succeeded with Charlie Chaplin. A crane
poised over the water extracts
a bus thru an ice hole, a solitary driver
plunged thru an hour or so before I woke.
Thoreau never lived, couldn't, to the fullest
beyond the borders of his own back pages
or the colonies of martins before a summer storm.
Did he love? why didn't he
wander the planet with his feet
like his mind? Car lights
line the incline of black hills at dusk.

Red lights right, white lights left,
deer live in tree groves beside the road
on the traffic-tied Cape Cod highway,
one long red line called Route 6
Kerouac never lived like his books
want, but never live, only teem
in possibilities he finds there
crossing a darkened yard of industry at dusk
in an after-work possibility, going
for the love of all things found
in his extinguished sensibilities
of the page now.

Leaves fall, the gray stone
walls visible again, only men
on bulldozers would try moving them.
My friend TV, I shut you off.
The Renaissance was a wonderful thing;
China had seven of them. Long dry grass by
a hydrant, two sparrows fly to safety as I pass.
Early bees in cold morning not
responding to glass tap. Oversize black eyes
atop tiny alien heads, they hunker to paper home
till sunlight slights the cold.
A critique of capitalism is not a blueprint for society.
A harrowing storm struck up between Harlem and Hartford.
A furious stillness hammers the landscape and
trees come alive, in voluminous shadows
by bleak pink light off silver highway poles
or from parking lots behind a stretch of trees.
Vertical grooves of cut stone remain free of accumulation,
make patterns in snow like black
pinstripes on a white field.

Once we knew we would die in fire
annihilation by bombs
and the handshaking men who made them.
Now if the water is drinkable, fishable,
we may see our children's children yet. Pale
blue snow tint visible in houselight gusts.
The many faces of the crowd represented in the mural,
some rubbed out of representation
in diversity's citywide eviction. The pediment
marred by shattered bottles of beer
the representative figure obscured
for lack of what is Pound there.
Orwell was right: a screen in every room.
Street corner littered by flower filled terra cotta pot
returned to terra firma from three stories up.
A tree in Boston bequeaths honor
to some sometime thugs of liberty. Some milk
poured onto sugar and crumbly flakes.

We choose kings, consider motives, wash
with warm water. The inferior status of the free man
is proof of genuine liberty. They wake,
inevitably rise, only to be used in war.
Only chiefs debate, hear criminal charges, transact
no business without being armed. Cormorants fly
high like tiny pterodactyls.

A Nuclear Bomb Is the Viagra of Nation-States

A nice black ant
walked about my kitchen sink
long after I finished breakfast.
Feeling humane, I tried to capture it
to release it from my domain.
In my haste and clumsiness I
crippled it with my fingers. It staggered
wildly, panicked, dragging crushed legs.
Feeling remorse but still optimistic
I threw it out the window,
wishing it well while it fell
to certain death. I read
for most of the afternoon, tinkered
on the piano, went for a walk, and
then read some more.

FRANK SINATRA IS DEAD

Shopping malls sprang up across the city
before the economic boom went bust
last year. They are a favorite target
of rioters. Most people were too poor
ever to shop there. The staff of
the International Monetary Fund
left Jakarta before dawn
on a chartered plane. At the fired malls
some people sifted ashes for things.

THE BEES

This, and my heart, and all the bees,
& a bush of flowers with the bees about them
& still more later flowers for the bees,
the little almsmen of spring-bowers.

Oscar Wilde found sweet fretful swarms of grumbling bees
& Tennyson the murmuring of innumerable bees.
Oh make us, Robert Frost, happy in happy bees.
The murmuring of Emily's bees has ceased.

One after one, the sound of rain and bees.
As from the hive where bees in summer dwell.

Myriads of bees
Yellow-girted bees
For winds to kiss
& grateful bees to feed. So
drunken reel her bees.
We should not mind
so small a flower.
Just when light of morn
with hum of bees, in
Keats, morning
flowers at song
of bees.

EVENT-RELATED BRAIN POTENTIALS

As if only a bicycle were destroyed
Instead of a man being killed
In the Netherlands, in Russia
As if I had forgotten the deliberate ear
The almanac of dactylics, thorns,
Sorrows, tales convey intaglio
Icons and artifacts prove popular among
Thieves to fight organized
Crime Germany permits
Electronic home surveillance
For the first time since the Nazi
Era Salman Rushdie is
Unimpressed at Khatami's proposal
An exchange of scholars, artists, writers,
And tourists as if the property
Foot print frost dies
In warpath ashes or headstone
Laments fit music hall appeals "I have
Nothing to be sorry for everything
I did was for love of the land of Israel," she smiles,
Waves to supporters, as if
Theorems, instructions, light-
House compositions the original
Reading fulfillment right now
It's thirty-nine degrees in the city at
A minute before ten o'clock
The Boston subway police
Vow to deal with "disorder"
Before 8 P.M. thirty cult members
Plan to kill themselves, repeat

By heart as if decay
In sneaking whispers
Passing mythology hardly ever
Obliterated, set in memory the new
End of the world coming
A space ship would pick their bodies up
From a mountain in the Canary
Archipelago a bear
On a Dakota air base
Mistaken for an invasion
As if business or the belly
Grapples amid troop mobilization
After the December massacre
Gravestone vagaries and laughter
Illustrate the moon away
Mute epitaph
Pluck sunset dollar
Down in Tokyo gold up in
London a thousand people murdered
Since the start of Ramadan the
Sawed off head
Of Copenhagen's little mermaid
Left at a TV station by a man wearing a hood
As if I was afraid it
Would all be gone
Irrepressible as love
Or labor, candles, couches
City light as if words
About nothing
A muffled
Reference
Or wind

IN THE COMPANY OF GOOD DOGS

In the company of dogs, two labs:
one black, the other brown. The black one
is a fetch junkie. I indulge her habit till the tennis
ball drips spit and sprays backward on a toss.

The brown one wants to hump the black one
but he's too relaxed about it and looks back
at me as if I could help him out. If dogs grin
he is grinning at me every time he fails to mount her.

It is late afternoon and I am drinking beer and being
perhaps too judgmental of others right now.
Two cardinals play chase around a scotch pine.
Two meadowlarks rough house in a clearing across the road.

Good dog, good dog. The brown one likes
his belly rubbed and the black one won't give it up,
ball clenched in her mouth, staring intensely
at me. She drops it before me and waits.

I ignore her and read. She sits,
a calculated act. As I grab the ball
she bolts for the woods and catches it
as it ricochets off a tree.

THE RELEASE

In his shoulders
diminutive revolutions

In his eyes
fear and faces
above him

Helpless fear
and helpless invocations

Go
your life was perfect
timing till tonight

Go, there's no water
anymore, no hearing

no crying,
go.

The Ducklings

Make way for the language
elicited from
illustrations in the books of children
drawn decades ago
in which antiseptic cities
suture a prosperous countryside.

Frost for the New Millennium

I'm going out to dredge the reservoir
I'll only stop to scrape the toxins away
(And measure uranium dust on the surface I may):
I shan't expose my skin long—you stay home.

EUROPEANS IN AMERICA

The starlings are tagged
with a continental title.
The swans are elegant
and mute. In Vermont
the swans are shot
for incompatibility
but the starlings
seem to be forever.

Audubon Days

for Kate Nugent

Algorithms, sunlight, and dark
dreaming, and reading, and dreaming,
going back and forth, snapping
string beans, scrubbing potatoes red from Maine.
Cartridges, clips, and pens:
nothing casually looted from small closet supplies.
Paper note pads, rubber bands:
I have at my hands the tools of each century.
Wordsworth, Caesar, and Jackson Mac Low.

The odes owed the Hudsonian godwit.

One of two great albatrosses
nests in the southern Pacific
and may attain a wingspan of eleven feet
but how many albatrosses
truly deserve to be called great?
Pushpins, cork board,
big tank of "prestige elite."

Blue jays and dickey birds.

The litany turned miscellany
a spring torrent of rent strike
bespoken of black crows
curled in mulch between brick wall and
thick trunk much like any other scared bird.
Starlings go at it with beaks of needle-nose pliers
shrieking and tearing at pizza thru tight saran.

Often acting like a chicken in the reeds.

Breeding coast to coast, the limit of tree lines,
the most common tit in North America.
Such was the stereo of activity
to the smallest bird. Titmouse indeed
does mean small bird.
Not holes in tooth
but the cavity of smaller trees
this female thinking about early spring early
and we thought she had forgotten,
appearances common as hunger
her wings in perch of departure
go looking for twigs in morning
who knows what you might get?

Studies show a richness of vocalization.

Impressive large King Penguin
reaches markets over three feet.
Similar employers stand a foot taller.
Penguins merge into colonies
may stray into the mainstream. Here
a pair of stockholders
engage in mirrored preening activity.
Odysseus did not
anger the gods with his pride,
He did
poke someone's eye out.

Told by adults not to beg from campers
poets develop a fondness for feeders.
Their needs are less than other birds

and often their hunger is a seed of grand works.
Not that an empty belly gets the job done
but the words need a sharp beak to break thru.
And many feeders lack mirrors.
Not that vanity ever preempted dinner
but the dishes were of a common manufacture.
Not that taste or reticence could supplant integrity.
Many times the fields feel empty.
Then a car
or a gunshot
sets things a-stirring.

I knew a girl who could sing as she read.

Adaptive, inquisitive, intelligent,
poets develop instincts for gutting Latinates
to their own wicked concerns. This is their best
quality they flitter and boast like any bird
in the grasses the big guys having become strong
or fat what's the difference? No eagle sacrifices
dignity for play. Why push forward if you cannot play?

The geese are waxing fat and sassy.

Beware the jackdaw's suspicions!
It muzzles along a stretch
near anything remote as malevolence
or paths leading you to it
endearing a gendarme along the way
they exist, gendarmes, they still do,
some are armed to the teeth
others cage about you with intent eyes
like a politician's, being polite all the while.

This bird paper I have written.

Bataleur tumble flight
but this is not about you.
I have no wingspan to speak of
or what I have is weak.
Drifting off half-dreaming in sleep
I hear the rhythms of day's talk,
its speech, inflections.
A tell-tail mocking bird
atop wall ledge with sparrows.
Small birds have small tails to tell.

Exasperation is the gaseous bag we're stuck with
and cannot properly pin stick.
Exoneration is something
Authority is careful for. Lynchpin
is the excuse we use after
forethought falls like a brick.

The Mycelium Concealed All Around Us

for Gerrit Lansing

Boletus versus
anamita. Growth
underground. Oak gall,
death cups and destroying angel.
Not the apple
of Peru that crippled Lane as a child,
his adulthood house remains, stripped
of neighborhood, a representative
romantic figure
sits in pollen fallen
from planted civic pines
and faces the harbor.
             Not the stinkhorn
(*phallus impudicus*), and not puff balls
feeding on damp trunks of dying trees, not even
the good tea-making staghorn sumac
smashed against rock. No, for us
whorehouses, dive bars, and used books.
And only the best of these. Chipped enamel,
dented colander, tattered collars, and average
cars.
             We work alone. We eat delicious
wild blueberries on the way, pull headrests
from bucket seats, run down Rockport
Sunday painters, and keep journals for everything:
each orgasm, hot meal, and adrenaline
rush. Blood runs from a fox's
open mouth as its head bobs

against the hunter's back. House lot
numbers beside ancient basements.
Hypha run like rhizomes for miles below paths
rupture in a proper climate
and die quickly
and for decades and more.
This town square is what it all looked like once,
what it may look like again
lost in company of bulbous toads
beside haunting interiors of terminal
moraines or amid birdland riots where bait
drops from a jetty.

GEANEALOCUS

Trestle beams settle into topography

Marquetry and rivets below state line

Freight value shifts upon crossing

The distance between two capital cities

Dozens of depots, stations, villages between

Not difficult ground, not intrepid walking

No ankle vexation in paced negotiations

Some small ravines resemble washed-out attempts

Water control stones stacked in slopes

Fallen detritus or drift firms cementing sediment

From the bridge a vista in generous scope

Trains across fields far in either direction

Altho desire imagines a century earlier

Preclude the woodshed boon now enormous and rural

Electricity displace populace concentration

Enable proximity a roadside consideration

Cars turn beeping into dark of stone tunnel

City road curve empties into pasture

Of factories, warehouses and now there's a prison

Near the foundries with felons imported from Texas.

Vinyl seats of trains are unsatisfactory

Speed beside bedside too close approximation

An appreciative view difficult in angling

Save when approaching, finally, your station

The conductor slides open the passenger door

And iron scrap flashes in passing waste yards

And gleaming stainless steel

Of grated steps you could throw yourself from

In auburn sunlight striking finite granite rocks

Neglected areas of administered lots, overgrown in green,

Heaped in soiled mattress and rubber tire

Pollutant listening in public has lessened

Hard won lessons of visibility management

SABLE ISLAND

All those tough old ponies
and disquieting stark

beach heads.

I have not been there.
Unfit they say
for people and rats, even concrete
pilings

sunk

      in sand, and roots

vines and wind-
rubbed rocks.

SHUT THE DOOR

You know how insects
get caught

inside the enormous rooms and
go insane

against glass panes
of huge windows.

How the fly sounds.
And bees and wasps.

You've seen the plain
wood chair

backed against the floorboard
beneath the window

and a smart small writing table
beside it.

THE EVENINGS

I used to love going out in the evening.
Depletion of gasoline linger and exhaust
of light, cement heat about the time
car lights coming on on the highway and
median lawn mown thick into summer.

I used to love that light imploding
trees in leaves' shadow in boon
of vertical sun. And the smell too
of charcoal lighter soaking maybe less so
than adhesive on plastic peeled away from its waxy paper.
I used to sit on the stoop while fireflies lit up
in and around bushes
                              while quivers of blue light
flickered from televisions along lines of red
brick row house living room windows
above a steady increase of singing crickets.
Headlights spun above my bed
like wing nuts on an oiled thread spin.

I used to love getting up in the morning
barefoot to step on hot blacktop driveway
toward significant material lives
left near garage doors and back doors
and the nose of a tied dog
exploring dew under a canopy of clandestine
bird calls. Then convulsive water spit forth
basement cool from a warm green hose.

REPETITIVE STRAIN

Walk toward sunlight on a cold day.
So much already to decide. Strange
that impeachment makes such little impression.
I guess we'll get what we deserve by Christmas
anyway. Leaves droop and stir, black against twilight's dim.
Things colored dully under halogen street lamps. I remain
unchanged but older;
the subjective, selective, forgetful past
drained of its sappy romantic aspect.
History, an odometer. This time as if
all our hearts would stop on the stroke of midnight
with the precision of a computer.

No, we'll drop dead quickly maybe,
or hang on for years
with a lot of time to think
(if we care to).

I've got a bit of arthritis in my forefinger
right now as I write.
Remember me.
I've got a slight dull throbbing pain in my finger,
sinews stretched like a rubber band,
reaching up the underside of my arm—the arm
I brush my teeth with twice a day.

CONSCIOUSNESS OF SELF

In my daydream I am smoking but never in my night-
dream am I smoking and sometimes driving a pretty
nice car tho I do not own a car nor do I smoke but
I am smoking in my introspective daydream, walking
the avenue, brooding along the river bank or sidewalk
and my hands are occupied, face is drawn, and in the car
sometimes my elbow on the door, sometimes "incognito"
and this occurs when I come up short in thought,
or disengage from the moment, rebuked in my imagination
for having come up short in response, opinionated or
silly, brash or indignant, dissenting I hate smoking I
think but if I did smoke I would be smoking right now.

I KNOW I AM HOME

Paris is what we'll always have.
Back in the States we have bacon,
two eggs, wheat toast.

I pull a five franc Eiffel Tower from my pocket
and place it on the counter
between us when you ask for tea and I
get coffee and two serious looking guys
come in and order coffee.

The metal clip rack by the bread
holds one ounce potato chip bags.
Small, medium, and large Styrofoam
cups display with magic
marker what it costs to go.

WATCHWORD HO

Westward they go, a quarter-million

that, or twice that
of a wet, rainy afternoon the
winter of 1846
our new home beyond all this
evidences of strong emotion
in pencil or blurred and shaped
entire landscapes take away the
bewildered to justify that invasion

without regard, legal
or otherwise considered
as being uncivilized
discovers like Adam, moves thru
some faint idea of green grass
up early and walk
on a good day the
Oregon Trail marks the end of
Great Plain
buffalo

A BRIDGE

Absence of light on the surface
Is a water right
And natural law whose loops
Thread electric reflection. You
Have what some
Call beautiful eyes
But you will never look
Into the same sky twice.
The river is wide, night
Is a game and the game
Of reverie is never fixed.